MIND

to

HEART

Motivational Thoughts

ANDREA CURRY, MHA, PhD

ISBN 978-1-64416-776-2 (paperback)
ISBN 978-1-64416-777-9 (digital)

Christian Faith Publishing, Inc.
832 Park Avenue
Meadville, PA 16335
www.christianfaithpublishing.com

Printed in the United States of America

Dealing with Delay and Disappointment

It is the Lord who goes before you; He will be with you. He will not fail you or abandon you. Do not fear or be dismayed. (Deuteronomy 31:8, AMP)

Disappointment is one of the sneakiest emotions that we have to manage. It can creep upon you in an instant and change your entire disposition. Learning how to deal with disappointment is a valuable skill that can help to invoke peace in your daily life. It is true that we are going to be disappointed, but it becomes dangerous when we find ourselves disappointed in God. Satan loves to make you feel neglected and forgotten just because you are experiencing a delay. We have become accustomed to everything happening quickly because of the world that we are living in. We get everything fast from food to communication. One of my favorite scriptures is Isaiah 55:8: "For my thoughts are not your thoughts, neither are your ways my ways, saith the Lord." Instead of giving in to a pity party, ask God what it is that He is trying to teach you while you wait. There is always a lesson in the delay of an answered prayer. One of the greatest methods of success for dealing with delay and disappointment is to focus your attention on an area that you can thrive in. Is there a need that you can meet for someone? Is there a friend in your life that could use a listening ear? It is never easy to deal with disappointment, but often when you find something else to occupy your time, the wait is not as challenging. Do not become consumed by your emotions simply because things are not happening according to your timetable.

Knowing When to Be Quiet

The one who has knowledge uses words with restraint, and whoever has understanding is even-tempered. Even fools are thought wise if they keep silent, and discerning if they hold their tongues. (Proverbs 17:27–28)

There is an art to speaking that so many of us struggle with. We feel like we have so much to say that sometimes we do not effectively know when to apply restraint by being quiet. Remaining quiet in times of intense anger, frustration, and disappointment is a best practice that we all should apply. Even when you are going through challenges, it is best to be very careful with what you say. You can learn more by being quiet than you ever will by talking. Be intentional with how you use your words. Just pause to determine if what you are saying is actually beneficial and necessary. When you use wisdom, you will be prevented from saying things that you may later regret. As a child, I was often told that when you talk too much, you are going to start lying. So the next time you are tempted with a good conversation that you know you should not be a part of, get quiet. Gossipers will soon find another outlet if they know you will not add anything to the conversation. When you are upset about something in your life, just take it to God in prayer. You do not even have to utter it aloud. What is so wonderful about God is that He can interpret our moans and groans. There is a blessing in being quiet. I encourage you to try this. Measure each thing that you say today and watch how it transforms your life!

When Quitting Is Not an Option

But as for you, be strong and do not give up, for your work will be rewarded. (2 Chronicles 15:7)

When God has ordained you to do something, you can never consider quitting. You cannot expect that your entire journey will not present obstacles. Obstacles are necessary to build our character and strengthen our faith. When you quit, you are simply telling God that you do not trust Him to bring you through. When you quit, you are merely proving to Satan how weak your belief is in God. When you quit, you are not being a true representative of a strong soldier. There are going to be days when you feel like it would just be better to simply walk away, but those are the days where you have to sincerely pray for more strength to keep fighting for what you believe in. God never allows us to be blessed in the beginning to fail at the end. You cannot quit. You have to keep going. You must push yourself to reach the next level through sheer determination and zeal. When God hands out assignments, He never includes caveats that quitting is an option. He already knows that you are going to be successful before you are ever presented with the opportunity to move forward. You are legitimately a winner!

God Restores

God, pick up the pieces. Put me back together again.
You are my praise! (Jeremiah 17:14, MSG)

Our well thought out lives are sometimes scattered about into little pieces. We stop in awe and often wonder how we got to that point. Things were going so well, and now it seems like we are scrambling to get through each day. When your life appears to be in disarray, remember that God can restore. The greatest example of this is found by reviewing the book of Job. Job lost everything that mattered to him, but he never once lost his hope that God would make everything right again in his world. Only God can fix what may seem to be broken in your life. One word from Him causes the storms to cease, the winds to calm, and clouds to depart. Have you ever stopped to think that maybe things are not working out because you are trying to do God's job? We think that we should be able to fix what appears to be messed up, but that is incorrect. Each time that you get out of His way, He gathers the pieces and creates a masterpiece. Can you still be faithful to God even when you do not understand what He is doing with the pieces of your life? Will you give Him the opportunity to make you whole both naturally and spiritually?

Heart Check

But the Lord said to Samuel, "Do not consider his appearance or his height, for I have rejected him. The Lord does not look at the things people look at. People look at the outward appearance, but the Lord looks at the heart. (I Samuel 16:7)

Our culture dictates that we pay strict attention to our physical appearance. We love our fashion, fitness, cuisine, and expressing ourselves. It becomes a problem when we put more emphasis on our outer appearance and neglect what is most precious—our heart. The heart cannot be seen based on how you look but rather how you behave. You show love with your actions. The heart can be full of ill intentions if you are not careful. The heart can abhor jealousy, deception, envy, pride, haughtiness, and evil. Every now and again, we should stop and ask God to examine our hearts. The heart dictates how we treat others. The heart is our compass for showing love with those around us. The health of a person always stems from the condition of the heart. Are you spiritually healthy? Is there something that you need to get right with someone? Are you holding on to unforgiveness? A sincere prayer involves inviting the Lord into our hearts on a continuous basis. Your level of success in this life does not matter at all to God if you heart is corrupt. "Create in me a clean heart, O God; and renew a right spirit within me" (Psalm 51:10).

Dig Deeper

Let your roots grow down into him, and let your lives be built on him. Then your faith will grow strong in the truth you were taught, and you will overflow with thankfulness. (Colossians 2:7)

Why are we so quick to throw in the towel when things do not seem to go the way we thought? We become inundated with feelings of helplessness because we are praying for miracles, but we are content with being slothful. If we are handed every blessing and receive every answer to our prayers, but we put forth no effort, what are we learning? The Biblical lesson in James 2:20 is something that we must apply to every goal that we hope to reach. Dig deeper when you feel like you are on the cusp of achieving something great. Refuse to throw in the towel just because the outcome is not happening like you envisioned. You should want to build your faith up so strong that no challenge weakens your resolve to succeed. Dig deeper through prayer and reading your Word when you feel like you might crumble. Each time that you can stand strong during turbulence is a testament of your strong roots in Christ. With each trial and test, dig deeper so that you will not falter when you have to weather the storms of life.

Leaning = Trusting

Trust in the Lord with all thine heart; and lean not unto thine own understanding. (Proverbs 3:5)

D o not become disappointed and frustrated when situations do not work out the way that you thought they should. Have you ever stopped to think that the outcome was dependent upon your outlook? I believe that God allows things to happen when we forget that we must lean on Him. Leaning equates to trusting because you realize that God has you. You do not have to stay up at night worrying about your future. You trust that God will not allow you to falter even when your path seems unclear and uncertain. There will be times when you must remember that you do not always have to be strong. Lean on the Lord when you are feeling weak in your faith. Trust in Him when you feel like you want to hang your head in defeat. You are not meant to rely upon your own strength. I encourage you today to give your burdens, problems, worries, and concerns all to God. Lean on Him to shift the weight that you have been carrying. Trust Him to lead you all the way to victory.

Finish Strong

Being confident of this very thing, that he which hath begun a good work in you will perform it until the day of Jesus Christ. (Philippians 1:6)

A tactic that the enemy loves to use is the spirit of defeat. When things do not go as we planned, we are tempted to throw in the towel. When observing others, it seems like they have it easy. We have to stay focused on what God is doing in our individual lives. I was instantly encouraged this morning when today's scripture resonated at the forefront of my mind. You never know what someone else is dealing with, but you can be assured that God has not forgotten about you. Everything that He has started to do in your life will continue to be a priority of our Father until the Day of the Lord. So there is no vision, dream, gift, or goal that He has allowed you to start that He does not intend to finish. He does not guarantee that things will work out according to our timetable, but His Word says that He will continue to work on our behalf. Make it up in your mind that you will keep going even when you get tired, down, frustrated, and unmotivated. Only you can decide to finish strong! Let's keep fighting the good fight of faith.

Learn the Lesson or Repeat It

Surely God is my help; the Lord is the one who sustains me. (Psalm 54:4)

Have you ever tried to approach your life experiences with the mindset that there is a lesson in everything that you go through? God wants to teach us how to depend on Him. He wants us to be assured that He is in control. Sometimes we are faced with challenges that seem like they are so overwhelming that we find ourselves weeping and praying for relief. Never forget that each time we go through something, there is a lesson. If you find yourself in the same situation time after time, then you have not have grasped what it was intended for you to learn. As we are being molded into the image of God, it is required that we pass certain tests. You cannot become an effective representative of the Lord without obtaining key principles regarding His sovereignty and omnipotence without going through certain challenges. The blessed hope is that you only have to learn what God is trying to teach you. How simple is that? Simply pass the test in order to not repeat the lesson. When you pass the test, you will be able to help others pass it as well. Never neglect to share how you made it through with someone going through a similar situation.

Be Faithful

If you are faithful in little things, you will be faithful in large ones. But if you are dishonest in little things, you won't be honest with greater responsibilities. (Luke 16:10, NLT)

The art of faithfulness is an area that most people are familiar with. Being faithful is most desirable and requires that one makes a commitment to do not only what is expected but to also go above the bare minimum. Faithfulness is an area where many believers become lackadaisical especially when petitions are made to God to "enlarge my territory." Your delay in reaching the next level might be the result of you not being faithful where you currently are. Sometimes we need to check our attitude about our current circumstances. For example, are you praying for a new job? How are you handling the blessing of employment right now? Are you giving your all to your projects and responsibilities? We cannot pray and ask God to bless us when we are not doing our part. Show Him that you can be faithful with more. Each day apply the mindset that you are going to be fully invested in each project that your hands touch. God does want to bless us and answer our prayers, but you have to give Him something to work with. Master the principle of faithfulness by properly managing everything entrusted to you!

Divine Setups

For I know the thoughts that I think toward you, saith the Lord, thoughts of peace, and not of evil, to give you an expected end. (Jeremiah 29:11)

Don't you just love it when God encourages you with His Word? The instances that we encounter in life that seek to rob us of our hope are countered by what God has already spoken over our lives. Whenever it is necessary, remind yourself that God does not ever set us up for failure. When you feel like you are going to falter, stop and reflect on the scripture above. Everything that you experience in this life has already been intricately planned and is a part of your divine destiny. When God blesses something, it is blessed from the beginning to the end. God never starts something that He does not intend to finish. Sometimes when life gets hard, it is a time to just relax in God. You do not have to stay up at night worrying or allow your peace to be stolen by fear. This is the time to thank God for blessing you to get to this point. With every road-block along the way, continue to thank Him for the divine setup that He is preparing you to experience.

It's Mine

Let us hold tightly without wavering to the hope we affirm, for God can be trusted to keep his promise. (Hebrews 10:23)

I t is time out for thinking that God has forgotten about you. His promises concerning your life are absolute! You must get to the point where you reject every notion that things are not going to happen for you. Delays are sometimes just a part of the process. God never sets us up for failure even when it seems like it is taking too long for things to manifest. We have a right to claim all of the blessings that are assigned to us. It is no longer acceptable to have pity parties by allowing Satan to make you doubt God. Satan's sole objective is to make you forfeit your future. Just like a little child, stretch your hand out to receive everything that is intended for you. I do not know about you, but I am claiming all that is for me will become my reality. Every dream and the vision that God has given me for my life is going to happen. You can do the same. If you want it, it is yours to claim!

Conquerors Never Quit

Nay, in all these things we are more than conquerors through him that loved us. (Romans 8:37)

Sometimes throwing in the towel seems like the most rational decision. Mounting frustration with current circumstances can become exasperating due to our inability to create a solution that will lead to peace. We must always reject the notion of quitting. You have to make up your mind to fight for what you believe you are destined to accomplish. If you believe that God led you to it, then keep fighting the good fight of faith (See 1 Timothy 6:12). We cannot only expect to experience only good in this life. There have to be periods of refinement and testing. What should give us hope is the fact that God's Word tells us that we are more than a conqueror. He knows that we are going to get weary, but we can overcome through Him. Nothing that we are faced with is too hard or impossible to conquer. The recipe for success is that you have to include the Lord. It is only through Him that we have the strength to reject the notion to quit. He alone equips us with the power to conquer!

He's a Keeper

You will keep him in perfect peace, Whose mind is stayed on You, Because he trusts in You. (Isaiah 26:3, NKJV)

When the pressures of life seem to be overwhelming, take refuge in the fact that God is a keeper. You do not have to mull over the things that cause you anguish. Most of our problems come from worrying about situations that we have no control over. Instead of getting worked up over mundane details, focus your thoughts on God's goodness. Do not allow your mind to disrupt your sense of peace. Each time that I give a problem over to God and allow Him to work it out, He does just that. Keeping your mind on the Lord shows our Heavenly Father that you trust Him to see you through the situation no matter how challenging it may be. He wants to keep you through grief, disappointment, hurt, frustration, and even anger. If you allow Him to, He will keep you even when you want to throw in the towel. You have to do your part and focus on Him. We can depend on Him to keep us through every situation that we are faced with. There is joy in discovering peace in Jesus.

Share If You Care

It is my pleasure to tell you about the miraculous signs and wonders that the Most High God has performed for me. (Daniel 4:2, NIV)

Whenever you are presented with the opportunity to share your testimony, it should bring joy to your heart. There is no greater feeling than knowing that you have the insight to lift the burden of someone else by encouraging them so that they feel like they can make it through their situation. Overcoming obstacles and reflecting on all God has done should make you thankful and willing to share that with someone going through a similar storm. God wants us to share of His goodness. What you survived was not for you, but it was for someone else who needs to hear about it. Do not be ashamed of your past experiences. Each hurdle conditions you to overcome what is ahead. If you care, share with others about how you survived heartache, unstable finances, death of loved ones, and turmoil on your job. Let others know about how you made it through a health crisis. You must share how you survived during those times. What did you do to remain full of faith despite what you were going through? What insight can you share that will make going through the process a little easier? How did you cope with seemingly impossible circumstances? What are some of your favorite scriptures that bring you comfort? Can you sacrifice some of your time to be a motivating source of strength for others? Be the light in someone else's world. Someone is depending on you to share how you made it through so they can do the same.

Pray Always

Rejoice always, pray continually, give thanks in all circumstances; for this is God's will for you in Christ Jesus. (1 Thessalonians 5:16–18)

Whenever you feel heaviness in your heart, take the time to stop and pray. Prayer is one of our greatest weapons as believers. It has the power to provide us with strength, direction, encouragement, and peace. When we pray, we have the opportunity and privilege of taking our burdens to God confidentially. He already knows about everything we are going through, but He desires to hear from us. Just think about how strong you will become when you make prayer a priority. Do not just call out to God when you are in distress. You should establish a relationship with Him. Prayer is our opportunity to communicate with Him. He wants to speak to you too. A peace that is unexplainable comes from releasing your burdens at the feet of the One who can ease them. Take everything to the Lord in prayer! He is waiting to hear from you.

Stand Strong

For as the heavens are higher than the earth, So are My ways higher than your ways. And My thoughts higher than your thoughts. For as the rain and snow come down from heaven, And do not return there without watering the earth, Making it bear and sprout, And providing seed to the sower and bread to the eater, So will My word be which goes out of My mouth; It will not return to Me void (useless, without result), Without accomplishing what I desire, And without succeeding in the matter for which I sent it. (Isaiah 55:9–11)

Don't you just love to hear about all that God has planned for your life? It brings us great joy to know that God wants to bless us in the areas that we have been praying about. It becomes challenging when it seems like God has forgotten about us and all that He said He is going to do. You can be assured that if God has decreed and declared that He is going to do something special in your life, it will come to pass. God is not like us; He does not change His mind once He speaks. Do not expect God to operate according to your personal timetable. Hold your head up and stand on His Word. His Word will always accomplish what He intends. Be encouraged today to hold on to that specific Word you received from The Father. It is going to manifest at the appointed time!

No Failure

Not only that, but we rejoice in our sufferings, know-
ing that suffering produces endurance, and endurance
produces character, and character produces hope, and
hope does not put us to shame, because God's love has
been poured into our hearts through the Holy Spirit
who has been given to us. (Romans 5:3–5)

We can sometimes become so inundated with success that we stumble when everything does not come easy. When things go awry, we feel like we have failed. There is something to be said for the individual that can praise God during both trials and triumphs. It is important that we experience delays because they prune our faith, our testimony, our witness, and our character. God loves us and knows that we will need to experience disappointment and challenges in order to cultivate us into the best representation of His character. One of the enemy's greatest tactics is to make us believe that we are a failure just because things may not have happened or worked out according to our own preconceived notions and plans. When those feelings rise up, and you feel like you have failed, cast those thoughts back into the very pits of Hell. You are never a failure in God. Encourage yourself with the mindset that you will keep working toward your goals. It may take you longer to achieve your ambitions, but remember that your life is a journey and not a marathon. You are a success in Jesus!

Your Words Matter

Let your speech be always with grace, seasoned with salt, that ye may know how ye ought to answer every man. (Colossians 4:6)

One of the most powerful tools that we should incorporate into our everyday lives is to pause and think before speaking. It is so unfortunate to encounter people in conversation who utter every single thought that they have without regard to how it may be received. We should always stop to measure our words to make sure that what we are saying is both helpful and edifying. One method to ensure that is to ask yourself if what you are about to say is really necessary. If we are not careful, we can tear people down with our words, and the damage is sometimes irreparable. In anger and frustration, always pause so that you will not create issues that can be avoided. We should never refrain from telling the truth to one another, but there is always a right way to do it. Be intentional with everything that you say. Speak in love and never neglect to practice restraint. Sometimes it is better to not say anything at all than to say what may be necessary at the wrong time. Choose to build up others with your words by demonstrating Christian love in every conversation.

Seasons

To every thing there is a season, and a time to every purpose under the heaven. (Ecclesiastes 3:1)

When life gets overwhelming, just remember that what you are going through is only temporary. When you stop to reflect on that principle, it should encourage you to endure in the season that you are in. Remind yourself that it will not always be this way when you are faced with situations that cause you discomfort. Embrace the lesson that you are to learn in each season. Instead of questioning God about why you are dealing with particular circumstances, ask God what He is trying to teach you. When your resources are limited, God is teaching you how to lean on Him. When you are in between employment, God is teaching you that He is your ultimate provider. When your health is attacked, He wants you to trust Him to be your healer. I have seen God do things that seemed impossible and turn things around in the nick of time. You may not understand why you are going through the season you are in, but remember that there is a purpose for every season. It may be hard, and we all have been there. Depend on God for wisdom, strength, and endurance to remain focused as you go through your assigned season.

Letting Go

Let all bitterness, and wrath, and anger, and clamour, and evil speaking, be put away from you, with all malice: And be ye kind one to another, tenderhearted, forgiving one another, even as God for Christ's sake hath forgiven you. (Ephesians 4:31–32)

One of the hardest things for us to do at times is to let go of our ill feelings and opinions regarding others. When we feel that we have been treated unjustly, it takes prayer to rid ourselves of unhealthy thoughts and actions. Sometimes we just want to set the record straight by calling attention to the issue with the offender. We feel justified by bringing up the topic of contention, but it honestly does not fix the situation. If anything, it just causes us to be angry and resentful. We have to recognize that confusion does not come from God. Our enemy, Satan, enjoys getting us upset over situations that only come to weaken our witness and test our patience. The best remedy for situations where you have been hurt is to take them to God in prayer. He alone can soften hearts and mend our wounds. God commands us to forgive without exception. If we pause before reacting, we will have peace instead of a spirit of revenge. So the next time that you are faced with a situation that is causing you anguish, get quiet. Take it to the Lord before discussing it with anyone. Ask Him to show you how to handle the situation in love even if you are not in the wrong. It takes real spiritual maturity to let things go and trust that God will handle them. As believers, we must always choose forgiveness even if letting go means that you have to walk away.

Be A Doer

All Scripture is inspired by God and is useful to teach us what is true and to make us realize what is wrong in our lives. It corrects us when we are wrong and teaches us to do what is right. God uses it to prepare and equip his people to do every good work. (2 Timothy 3:16–17)

Many of us take the time to read God's Word on a consistent basis, but are our lives a true reflection of what the Bible says? Growing up, I always heard after the scripture was read in church, "May God add a blessing to the reader, hearer, and doer of His Holy Word." There is a blessing in not only reading and hearing The Word but also doing what it says. If you read the Bible but refuse to apply its principles, it is the equivalent of having an instruction manual needed to assemble a product. If you do not use the manual, your finished product will probably not be as the manufacturer intended. If you choose not to use our manual, the Bible, like it is intended, you will exist, but you will forfeit experiencing all that God has planned for your life. You should want to be a doer of God's Word. Living a life based on His principles will allow you to experience His blessings. Doing things His way will only enrich your life. We will be held accountable for all of the Word that we heard and read that we chose to not obey. May each of us strive to be a doer which ultimately pleases the Lord.

It's Not Your Battle

The Lord shall fight for you, and ye shall hold your peace. (Exodus 14:14)

We find ourselves dealing with unnecessary problems when we try to assume the wrong position. We instinctively want to jump the gun and handle things that God already has in control. I love it when He encourages me with "Peace be still." An unexplainable calmness immediately takes over my heart and mind. If you want to win the battle, let the Lord do the fighting. When you are faced with situations that tempt you to lash out, be still. It takes real maturity to not respond to everything that is presented to you. You do not have to clear your name, plead your case, or offer explanations. Just be still and let God work it all out. The truth always wins. Darkness is always overshadowed by light. It can be hard to sit still when you really want to garb up in your battle gear. It is not your battle. Do not prematurely act out and create a bigger mess. Sit down and be still. You will be amazed at how God works things out when you simply obey His Word. He cannot fight for you if you are already throwing punches. Always let Him handle it if you truly want to experience victory.

For His Glory

*Be exalted, O God, above the heavens, And Your
glory above all the earth. (Psalm 108:5)*

When God allows us to successfully make it through a
trial, we have a responsibility to tell of His goodness.
So many times while we are in the "wilderness," we cry
out to God to deliver us from whatever is causing us affliction. There
is nothing wrong with that, but we cannot neglect to give Him the
glory once we are delivered. Your passing of the test always gives you
an opportunity to give God the glory. Thank Him for giving you the
strength and the mind to lean on Him when you did not know how
things were going to work out. Give Him the glory for turning things
around and giving you a different outcome. Never neglect to give
Him all the praises that are due because you did not bring yourself
out, heal your body, increase your finances, or ease the burdens on
your heart. When we give Him the glory, it pleases Him. We have
to remember that it is *not* about us, but our lives should be *all* about
Jesus!

Agape Love

"Teacher, which is the greatest commandment in the Law?" Jesus replied: "Love the Lord your God with all your heart and with all your soul and with all your mind. This is the first and greatest commandment. And the second is like it: Love your neighbor as yourself." (Matthew 22:36–39)

Love always requires action. In our current society, the word "love" is tossed about so casually. Agape love involves sacrifice. Our greatest example of this type of love is what Jesus did for us on Calvary. As humans, we do not use agape love to describe how we feel about each other. We are not required to demonstrate love the way that Jesus did, but He did tell us how to love each other. Would you gossip about yourself? Would you betray your own confidence? Would you intentionally hurt your own feelings? Would you wish ill upon yourself? No, you would not. We only want the best for ourselves. So love others just as much as you love yourself. Be concerned about the well-being and spiritual health of others. Be quick to meet needs that you see. Be compassionate. Be genuine. Be real. Be willing to sacrifice your time and resources in order to help someone else. Do not just be a talker; be a doer. Love only stated and not demonstrated is a contradiction. Love completely and without selfish intention. Love is the only way!

His Way Is Always Right

But Naaman became angry and stalked away. "I thought he would certainly come out to meet me!" he said. "I expected him to wave his hand over the leprosy and call on the name of the LORD his God and heal me!" (2 Kings 5:11)

So many times we have our own ideas regarding how things are going to work out in our lives. We pray asking God to handle situations regarding our health, our finances, our relationships, and our careers. We become disappointed when God does not work things out the way that we hoped. Sometimes our breakthrough is dependent upon our obedience to do what He said. In the text, Naaman was healed when he obeyed and dipped seven times in the Jordan River. Naaman learned a powerful lesson that we should all apply to our lives: always obey. You cannot pray to Him saying, "Lord deliver me" while refusing to do what He said in order to experience freedom, deliverance, and healing. You may not understand why He said to do this or that, but remember that His way is always right! We have to trust His wisdom and depend on Him for guidance. There is always purpose behind His instructions. You cannot ask Him to move if you insist on wearing cement shoes.

Molded

But now, O Lord, thou art our father; we are the clay, and thou our potter; and we all are the work of thy hand. (Isaiah 64:8)

There is something so significant about realizing that who you are has absolutely nothing to do with your personal ideals. Each of us were uniquely created with a predetermined destiny. In order to be successful in life, we have to allow God to mold us. He molds us through periods of refinement that are often uncomfortable and confusing. Clay requires that the potter guides its shape through constant hand movements. We should think of our lives the same way. When we allow Our Father to be the potter, we should never think that He has removed His hands. He is consistently there guiding you through life. Each hardship that you experience is simply another opportunity for you to become more malleable. With each twist and turn, clay never breaks but rather continues to change its shape as the potter moves their hands. Allow God to mold you into what He desires for you to become. Do not fall into the trap of thinking that you know more than the Potter because you know the shape that you want your life to take. Always remember that the Potter knows best. His vision for His clay is always for it to form into the most beautiful reflection of His heart. You may not understand, but He is molding you into what He wants you to be!

Scars

But he was wounded for our transgressions, he was bruised for our iniquities: the chastisement of our peace was upon him; and with his stripes we are healed. (Isaiah 53:5)

Scars are merely a testament of God's goodness. What you encountered may have caused you pain and discomfort, but it did not kill you. Sometimes we can allow our scars to hold us back from experiencing future blessings. One thing about scars is that you have to deal with them. If you do not attend to a scar, it will leave proof that you were hurt. What is so amazing is that with a little tender loving care, the evidence of the scar can be diminished. Everything that we will go through in this life has already been conquered by Christ. We are healed already from everything that may present itself in our lives. So if it is grief, sickness, betrayal, abandonment, theft, or jealousy to name a few, you are already healed. Our Father says that you are healed so walk in it. You went through it because He knew you were strong enough to endure the challenge. Allow healing to come into those wounds so that you can experience freedom.

Now Faith

Now faith is the assurance (title deed, confirmation) of things hoped for (divinely guaranteed), and the evidence of things not seen [the conviction of their reality—faith comprehends as fact what cannot be experienced by the physical senses]. (Hebrews 11:1)

Have you ever had a situation where you wondered, "Where is God?" What if I told you that God is waiting on you to move on your behalf? That may sound preposterous to some, but it is a tried and true method. There is no such thing as possessing faith without a measure of works. How can you pray for God to do something for you, but you are unwilling to do anything for yourself? Yes, we should always wait with expectant hope for God to move in our lives, but we must be proactive as well. One thing I love about God is that He loves us so much and wants what is best for us. He does not want us to worry. So many times in our lives, we choose fear over faith, worry over joy, doubt over belief, and sadness over happiness. It's time for us to have faith that is so strong that nothing that we face causes us to lose heart. When the circumstances seem so dire that you do not see how you are going to make it, dig just a little deeper and remind God of His Word. We can find assurance in Hebrews 13:5 where He promised, "I will never leave thee, nor forsake thee." You can depend on Him. Just give Him something to work with. Raise your level of faith today!

How to Go Through

For I the Lord your God keep hold of your right hand; [I am the Lord], Who says to you, "Do not fear, I will help you." (Isaiah 41:13)

Did you know that there is a correct way to go through life's challenges? You can either accept your current circumstances and trust God through the process, or you can complain along the way. The most effective method to go through is to watch what you speak in the atmosphere when you are dealing with situations that are bigger than you. To be successful only speak what you want to occur. You should say, "I am healed. I am debt free. I am the lender, and not the borrower. My best days begin now." I dare you to try replacing negative words with positive ones. Complaining and whining may sometimes seem like a good idea due to frustration, but it really is pointless. Channel your energy into praise and thanksgiving by not focusing on what you are dealing with. Do not hinder your victory by your behavior while you are in the midst of situations that seem to be difficult. I have personally seen God turn things around for me when I have changed my perspective and response. Realize that He is right there with you and wants to help you. Are you going to commit to go through the right way? Praise Him for being right there beside you guiding you through the storms of life. Before you know it, that situation will be a distant memory that you can use as a testimony!

Just Speak It

For verily I say unto you, That whosoever shall say unto this mountain, Be thou removed, and be thou cast into the sea; and shall not doubt in his heart, but shall believe that those things which he saith shall come to pass; he shall have whatsoever he saith. (Mark 11:23, KJV)

K nowing and applying God's Word are two totally different things. We can read the text and still not believe that it actually works in everyday life. So many people go through life claiming to be a "believer," but yet doubt God's Word. The essence of the Christian walk is built upon the principle of faith. We believe not according to what we see, but what we know through our experiences with The Father. I challenge you to start proclaiming with your mouth everything that you want to accomplish this year. Instead of speaking negatives about your situation, start speaking positive. If you are believing for healing in your body, speak it. If you are believing for breakthrough in your life, speak it. If you are believing for new opportunities, speak it. Now the caveat is that you cannot simply speak it, but you must believe it in your heart! So the recipe for success is to speak and not doubt. "Death and life are in the power of the tongue, and those who love it and indulge it will eat its fruit and bear the consequences of their words" (Proverbs 18:21, AMP). Be careful with your words because they shape the course of your life.

He's Omnipresent

*The eyes of the Lord are in every place, beholding the
evil and the good. (Proverbs 15:3)*

One of the key characteristics of our Heavenly Father is His
ability to be with each of us at the same time. No matter
where we are and despite the number of us that call out to
Him simultaneously, He is more than able to be whatever we need
Him to be. We should be so thankful that we do not have to stand
in line or pull a number to get to His throne. We can just call out to
Him from our hearts with genuine and expectant hope that He does
hear us. When we encounter situations that are either good or bad,
we should be assured that God sees it all. We have an advocate that
is right there fighting our battles even before we utter a single word.
From the person in the hospital, to the inmate in prison, to the judge
in the courtroom, He is there. Even when situations come before
you that catch you off guard, know that God is still there. It is in the
times when we do not have an answer and cannot understand with
our earthly minds, that is when His omniscient presence manifests.
Give Him glory!

Just Trust

Trust in the Lord with all your heart and lean not on your own understanding. (Proverbs 3:5)

The Merriam-Webster dictionary defines trust as the assured reliance on the character, ability, strength, or truth of someone or something. Why is it so hard to trust God? Is it because we choose to not remember what He has already done in our lives? When we go through various tests and trials, we should use those experiences to not only use it as a resource to build our faith but to also encourage others. When you have come out of a hard situation, stop to reflect upon the lesson that you learned. It is so easy to trust when things are going well. It takes true spiritual maturity to trust when you do not know how things are going to work out. When you are wondering how you are going to pay your bills, feed your family, and maintain your livelihood, that is when we have to rely upon what we know about God. It does not matter what it looks like, trust anyway. When everything seems to be turbulent and uncertain, dig deep and raise your level of expectation. We can trust God to complete what He has begun in us. We can be assured of His character that if He has spoken something concerning our lives, it will come to pass.

No Looking Back

Brothers and sisters, I do not consider myself yet to have taken hold of it. But one thing I do: Forgetting what is behind and straining toward what is ahead. (Philippians 3:13, NIV)

Moving forward requires that you do not allow the experiences of your past to hold you back from grasping all that God has for you. It is preposterous to simultaneously focus on things that are in front of you and behind you. Since that is the case, doesn't it make the most sense to keep your attention on what is ahead of you? So many people allow the negative experiences from their past to keep them from maximizing the current opportunities that have been presented. So what if that relationship went sour, that job ended, you were looked over for that promotion, or you didn't meet your personal goals? Do not allow what you deem as failures to cause you to miss out on your future blessings. Instead of viewing the challenges as hindrances to success, use them as positive motivation for your current aspirations. You should deal with the feelings that disappointment brings whether it was a result of your decisions or someone else's. Press on to what lies ahead in your future. Cast aside all negativity and maintain forward vision. You have to let go of the past to embrace your future.

A Secret Keeper

A gossip betrays a confidence, but a trustworthy person keeps a secret. (Proverbs 11:13)

How many times have you shared something with someone by prefacing it with, "Now this is between you and me?" That small disclaimer gives one assurance that what will be shared will remain between the parties involved in the conversation. Too often trust is freely given without doing a background check on the heart of the recipient of our secrets. Samson was unknowingly betrayed by the woman he loved simply because he made the decision to share the secret regarding his strength with her (Judges 16). (Lesson: Do not allow your feelings to cloud your judgment regarding someone's character.) There is something so rewarding about being a person that can be trusted. Our greatest example is Christ. Whatever you share with Him in secret will always be treated as sacred information. He is the ultimate secret keeper. We should always strive to emulate His character. He always makes time for us. He is never too busy, and we are always a priority to Him. He wants to hear from us. All relationships are built on communication, and our relationship with The Father is no exception. Talk to Him. He already knows the ins and outs of your heart and thoughts, but He longs to be your secret keeper. You can trust Him with everything.

No Fear

So do not fear, for I am with you; do not be dismayed, for I am your God. I will strengthen you and help you; I will uphold you with my righteous right hand. (Isaiah 41:10, NIV)

When God makes the way clear for us, we do not have to fear about walking into what He has ordained. The problem with faith walking is that sometimes you stumble because of familiarity with your current set of circumstances and surroundings. You stop to wonder, "Lord, is this you?" instead of just trusting His provision. It is time out for us living in fear. When God is in something, He makes the way easy to walk right in. The thing that I love about God is that when He moves, He does everything perfectly. When He moves, there is no chance for anyone else to take His credit. He knows just when and how to bless His children. In order to be ready to receive all that He has for you, determine your level of preparedness. If He opened the door that you were secretly praying about, would you hesitate to move forward? We must refuse feelings of fear when we choose to follow God's direction. Fear is not of God, but it is a tactic of our enemy, Satan. Shake the chains of fear today and know that God is on your side ready to lead you right into your destiny!

Never Forget

Bless the Lord, O my soul, and forget not all his benefits. (Psalm 103:2)

One of the greatest methods that is used to paralyze faith at work is convenient spiritual amnesia. It is easy to think that the situation that you are in is so insurmountable that you will never come out of it unscathed. It is our responsibility as a believer to always remember the countless ways that He has made for us. We cannot forget that there are benefits to serving Him. Through our love relationship, He offers us protection, provision, guidance, peace, joy, and love. We should continuously thank Him for all He has done and what He will do. We bless Him by never downplaying the ways that He has made, the doors He has opened, and the hearts that He has softened for us. Going through certain challenges should cause us to keep those benefits at the forefront of our minds. Use your memory as a source of encouragement to counter the temptation of untimely forgetfulness.

Luck Involves Happenstance

We toss the coin, but it is the Lord who controls its decision. (Proverbs 16:33)

So many people entertain the misconception that luck is real. Nothing that occurs in your life is by accident or outside of God's view. Everything always happens just as it is supposed to. Refuse the temptation to be a background manipulator by trying to control things that you were never intended to have a hand in. You can make all the plans that you want, but always remember that God has the final say. It is so easy to take chances, but if we trust God, luck isn't necessary. Luck involves circumstantial occurrences. If this is done, then that might be the outcome. Life is so much better when we stop trying to hinder Him from what He does best. Remember that He sees the end from the beginning. As believers, we do not and should not believe in luck but rather choose to place our hope in Christ alone because we can trust that He always has our best interest at heart.

Tunnel Vision

Keep your eyes on Jesus, who both began and finished this race we're in. Study how he did it. Because he never lost sight of where he was headed—that exhilarating finish in and with God—he could put up with anything along the way. (Hebrews 12:2a, MSG)

When you study the life of Jesus, you will see how determined He was from the beginning of His ministry assignment. He knew who He was and what He was expected to accomplish. He did not allow naysayers and doubters to hold Him back. So many times, we doubt what God has said concerning our lives because we have taken our eyes off of Him by instead choosing to focus on other people. When you have the assurance that what you are doing is aligned with God's Will for your life, nothing and no one will be able to stop you. Put on your spiritual binoculars today and fix your gaze on Jesus when it seems like the race is too long or too hard. Never lose sight of what you are trying to accomplish by pursuing your purpose. So no matter what comes your way, see yourself on the other side. If God has allowed it, there is already a way made for you to get to the finish line. Our Lord is the greatest example of tenacity in the face of adversity. Narrow your vision to experience the victory!

Judgment Free Zone

You hypocrite, first take the plank out of your own eye, and then you will see clearly to remove the speck from your brother's eye. (Matthew 7:5)

I t is so easy to pinpoint the downfalls of everyone else, but when the time comes to acknowledge our personal shortcomings, it usually becomes challenging. It is so easy to draw attention to others because it can sometimes make you feel better about yourself. The problem is that you start to compare yourself to the other person because they do this or that, and you don't. If you care about someone, you should want to help them recognize reckless behavior that can have earthly and eternal consequences. Recognizing that we are all infallible requires that we humble ourselves to accept that we are imperfect. It is dangerous to never feel compelled to shine the spotlight on our own hearts, intentions, attitudes, and behaviors to search for ways to improve. Each day of our lives, we should strive to be better than the day before. We should want to always help those connected to us but not at the expense of putting ourselves on a pedestal. If you are quick to find fault with your neighbor, it would behoove you to determine what areas of your own life could use some tweaking. Always remember that there is only one true judge that sits on His throne, and He doesn't need our help. Love unconditionally even if you do not agree. Judge not and love more.

A Firm Foundation

❦

For he will be [nourished] like a tree planted by the waters, That spreads out its roots by the river; And will not fear the heat when it comes; But its leaves will be green and moist. And it will not be anxious and concerned in a year of drought Nor stop bearing fruit. (Jeremiah 17:8)

Before any building is constructed, the foundation is established. A firm foundation has to be able to bear the weight of the structure that will be built on top of it. Remember that no one is exempt from going through times of testing. As a Christian, our foundation is our relationship with the Lord. If you want to know how firm your foundation is, evaluate how you endure the storms of life. If your foundation is not steady, you will bend and break when your faith is tested. When you have a firm foundation, you always know within your heart that God will work it out. You can stand strong like a tree whose roots are so grounded that no strong wind will be able to snap it. Be like a strong tree that stands proud when the sun shines, the rain pours, the hail falls, and the wind blows. Endure each season like a tree with your limbs outstretched upward as a total surrender to God with the assurance of being rooted and planted.

Bask in His Glow

May the Lord smile on you and be gracious to you.
(Numbers 6:25)

According to published studies, sunshine improves moods. When the sun shines after it has been cloudy all day, it brings happiness to most that experience it. It is easy to get bogged down by the pressures of life which can cause worry and frustration to manifest. It is not always easy to portray peace during times of difficulty, but it can be accomplished by shifting our focus to the Son. Having joy deep within allows others to see Him shining in, on, and through us. Every day of our lives should be a reflection of His love through our thoughts, words, and actions. Do not allow things that are out of your control cause you to live down in the doldrums. Lift up your head and look up because the Son is brightly shining. He wants you to feel His glow and bask in His love. Allow the Son to radiate in your life, and you will experience unexplainable joy!

Run Your Race

*Don't you realize that in a race everyone runs,
but only one person gets the prize? So run to win!
(1 Corinthians 9:24)*

It always helps to keep your eyes on the finish line when you are running a race. You cannot successfully run your best if you are trying to watch the people around you. You will mess up every time! Life is the same way. We cannot go through life preoccupying ourselves with what everyone else is doing. Living your best life now involves being happy with what you currently have and resolving to work harder to achieve your personal goals. Your race may be more like a slow jog instead of a quick sprint. It may take you longer to get to your desired destination, but the most important thing is that you keep moving. You will have hurdles to overcome during this race, but it is up to you to dig deep to get over them. Aim to win in every area of your life by adjusting your focus and staying in your assigned lane. Remain within the parameters of what you have been called to do. You cannot claim the prize if you do not run. You cannot win if you do not begin. You have already been given the grace to run your race!

Embrace Your Season

I am not saying this because I am in need, for I have learned to be content whatever the circumstances. (Philippians 4:11)

During the childhood years, there is often the anticipation of being "grown." What is often overlooked is that there will be new challenges during that season such as living independently and paying bills. Once the wonder of being an adult has passed, there is often the desire to experience being a carefree child again. Unfortunately, that mentality follows us around in other areas of our lives if we are not careful. We start wondering and wishing that we could have this and that instead of enjoying the current moment. What we must remember is that when the season passes, we cannot go back. God put this on my heart to tell you to just embrace your season. It might be a challenging season, or one filled with joy. It might be a season of plenty or one of lack. No matter where you find yourself on the spectrum, take charge of your emotions, perspective, and outlook today. From this point forward, be content and enjoy where you are at this moment. Make the most of your current season with a healthy dose of expectant hope that even if this is not your best season, it will eventually come into fruition. Choose to believe that the best is still yet to come!

Now Is the Time

We plan the way we want to live, but only God makes us able to live it. (Proverbs 16:9)

It is amazing to see the number of people that go through life with no regard for God. Decisions are hastily made without seeking His guidance. Often ignored and placed on the back burner, He is still there graciously allowing blessings to occur for those who fail to acknowledge Him. Proverbs 3:5–6 says, "Trust in the Lord with all thine heart; and lean not unto thine own understanding. In all thy ways acknowledge him, and he shall direct thy paths." We must unequivocally give our full attention to God and His desires for our lives. It is time for us to turn away from living as if we are really in control. It is only because of Him that we have the strength to rise each day and handle the tasks assigned to us. We cannot afford to take life or our opportunities for granted. There is nothing wrong with making plans, but the error is made when we neglect to reverence Him in the process. If you want to experience true victory in every area of your life, consult Him in all of your decision-making. Realize that even though He already knows, He wants you to trust Him enough to share your plans. Now is the time to put God back in His place as the true head of our lives.

Drop the Weight to Elevate

Wherefore seeing we also are compassed about with so great a cloud of witnesses, let us lay aside every weight, and the sin which doth so easily beset us, and let us run with patience the race that is set before us. (Hebrew 12:1)

Before boarding a flight, your luggage has to meet certain criteria. Carry-on bags must fit in the overhead compartments, and checked luggage cannot exceed fifty pounds. If your checked luggage is over the allowed weight, you will be asked to remove some of the items. The extra items removed will allow you to proceed to the gate to board your flight. Life is the same way. We have to put aside the extra weight in our lives that prevents us from experiencing elevation. Your weight may be pride, anger, frustration, bitterness, unforgiveness, jealousy, envy, hatred, low self-esteem, or other people. Each of us has to make a decision regarding our future. Is that unnecessary weight that you are carrying worth you forfeiting your destiny? There is a divine peace that comes with lightening your load. Allow nothing and no one to cause you to remain stagnant. It's time to elevate. Your next level is waiting!

He Has Risen!

But on the first day of the week, at early dawn, the women went to the tomb bringing the spices which they had prepared [to finish anointing the body]. And they found the [large, circular] stone rolled back from the tomb, but when they went inside, they did not find the body of the Lord Jesus. (Luke 24:1–3)

Why do we sometimes doubt what God tells us? Prior to His death on the cross, Jesus told the women that He would be crucified and would rise on the third day. When that day came, they went searching for Him. Two angels had to remind them of what Jesus told them back in Galilee (Luke 24:4–8). We must never forget what He says because when He speaks, it shall come to pass. When He rose, He proved to His disciples that all they had to do was believe. They walked and talked with Him but were fearful when what He spoke came to pass. We have hope and joy today because He rose. He took away the fear of death and disease. He rose and is shining in the heart of every believer. He rose so that we can stand. We stand bearing the banner of salvation for all to see. He is alive and well. The story did not end on that rugged cross. He assumed His place in glory so that we can have the same opportunity. He rose from the borrowed tomb. Rejoice! Jesus lives.

No Limits

Now unto him that is able to do exceeding abundantly above all that we ask or think, according to the power that worketh in us. (Ephesians 3:20)

Isn't it so comforting to know that God sees the end of situations from the beginning? He does not need our permission to bless us, but we cannot limit God by trying to give Him our timelines for when we want things to happen for us. We make mistakes when we try to manipulate situations for our benefit because we think that we know what is best. The delayed manifestation of blessings is often because of our attitude, perception, and outlook regarding the situation. Are you willing to hand over the reins and totally trust God's wisdom? Every time that you can humble yourself to tell Him, "God, I trust you even though I do not see how this is going to work out," shows that you are not confining Him to your will. In the waiting period, continue to encourage yourself through the reading of your Word and prayer time. Thank Him in advance for the opened doors, new opportunities, and answered prayers. Jesus said in Matthew 19:26, "With men this is impossible; but with God all things are possible." Always remember that impossibilities are anomalies with our God!

Check Your Fruit

You can identify them by their fruit, that is, by the way they act. Can you pick grapes from thornbushes, or figs from thistles? (Matthew 7:16, NLT)

Have you ever gotten a piece of fruit that looked good on the outside, but you later discovered that the inside was rotten? If your spiritual heart was examined today, what would be found? Are you jealous or envious of others? Do you have malicious intent toward anyone? Are you mean and spiteful? Are you full of discontent and deception? Does your common practice involve being vengeful and vindictive? It is true that God alone truly knows the contents of the heart, but He admonishes each of us in 2 Corinthians 13:5 to examine ourselves. You should not only examine yourself, but you should also evaluate the fruit that you associate with. Always use discernment when forming new relationships and partnerships. Do not ignore the warning signs when you encounter and are exposed to bad fruit. Benjamin Franklin said, "The rotten apple spoils his companion." Just because it looks good, does not mean it is good. Bad fruit can only imitate good fruit short-term. The rotten core will always be exposed if you look closely. A good examination on the front end will always prevent future turmoil.

Attitude Adjustment

Give thanks in all circumstances; for this is God's
will for you in Christ Jesus. (1 Thessalonians 5:18)

Have you ever done something nice and considerate for someone, but they neglected to say, "Thank you?" The blatant indifference usually causes you to assess the recipient of the good or service. Now, how often are you guilty of treating the Lord that way? Doesn't He make ways for you, answer your secret prayer requests, protect you, and cause elevation to occur in your life? When was the last time you thanked Him? We should never believe that what we accomplish and experience is based on our own merit. It is because of Him that things are going as well as they are. We must always give God the credit and thank Him for all that we are blessed to experience. He does not have to do anything for us, but He chooses to continually bless us. It is simply erroneous and irresponsible to take our blessings for granted. If you notice that your attitude is leaning more toward entitlement instead of gratitude, choose to make the necessary adjustment today!

Unselfish Love

For Christ also suffered once for sins, the righteous for the unrighteous, to bring you to God. He was put to death in the body but made alive in the Spirit. (1 Peter 3:18)

Our Lord was falsely accused, beaten, pierced, mocked, nailed, and ultimately rejected by those who claimed to love Him. He went through all of that for us. He paid the price for our sins so that we could have eternal life. Good Friday is a reminder of Jesus's unselfish love. He knew He did nothing wrong, but He chose to suffer without complaining. How many times do we do something for others only because we are looking for something in return? When we think of true love, we should always think of the cross. He not only died for the believer but also those that do not believe. When He got on that cross, He knew that more than two thousand years later, He would still be rejected. He chose to stay there anyway. That's love! "Greater love hath no man than this, that a man lay down his life for his friends" (John 15:13). Each of us has an opportunity to not only appreciate His sacrifice but to also love each other unselfishly. Remember that He made a choice to suffer and die so that you could live!

Faith in Action

In the same way, faith by itself, if it is not accompanied by action, is dead. (James 2:17)

Faith is not the equivalent of paralyzed hope. Faith requires active participation. The Bible tells us that in order to be successful, we have to accompany works with our faith. Anything that we want to achieve in life is going to require that we do something to bring it to fruition. Do not get confused and think that you can just sit back and wish for things to happen for you. A popular basketball player warms up for over twenty minutes before each game and shoots over 120 shots. He takes the time to prepare for the victory he wants to experience. We should be the same way. Invest the time and effort in the areas of your life that you want to be successful. I truly believe that God is moved when we show Him that we want what we are praying for. Fill out that application, go test drive that dream car, and go look at that new home. Always remember that faith coupled with works equates success. Are you willing to do the prework?

Learning How to Wait

I wait for the Lord, my whole being waits, and in his word I put my hope. (Psalm 130:5)

Waiting is sometimes one of the hardest things for us to do. Waiting requires patience and determination to not give up when we experience delays. What if I told you that sometimes your blessings are held back because of your disposition while you are waiting? How many times have you prayed about something, and when it did not happen in the timeframe you thought it should, you became exasperated, irritated, and downright cantankerous? We must remember Isaiah 55:8, "For my thoughts are not your thoughts, neither are your ways my ways, saith the Lord." He knows each of us better than we could ever imagine. He knows when and how to bless us. He even knows when we will be best prepared to receive the answers to our prayers. So while you are waiting, guard your heart and your attitude. Wait with expectancy, hope, and patience. Trust that He does have your best interest at heart. Show Him that you trust His divine wisdom by practicing self-control while you wait.

The Courage to Fight

The Lord himself goes before you and will be with you; he will never leave you nor forsake you. Do not be afraid; do not be discouraged. (Deuteronomy 31:8)

Individuals that are serious about winning take the time to study their opponent. To ensure success, one must learn all about the strengths and weaknesses of the competition. Our true enemy, Satan, is roaming about waiting for the right opportunity to disrupt peace, steal joy, kill faith, and destroy hope (See John 10:10). Do not idly sit back and allow him any space in your mind or heart. One of the ways that he comes in is by planting seeds of doubt. He loves for you to question what God has promised you. He wants you to just throw in the towel when times get hard. If you want to defeat him, square your shoulders back, put on your armor, and put him back in his place. Those dreams that you have regarding your life are not just fantasies—they can become a reality. Fight for your goals and aspirations. Do not allow Satan to make you question your purpose. You can accomplish what is in your heart. It is really a matter of how bad do you want it, and are you prepared to fight courageously to get it?

Intentional Leadership

*In everything set them an example by doing what
is good. In your teaching show integrity, seriousness.
(Titus 2:7)*

As Christians, we are called to be leaders by living a life of integrity based on key biblical principles. Effective leadership is always conveyed by example. You cannot lead and desire to be a follower. Intentional leaders are not intimidated by others that want to emulate their methods for success. Real leaders confidently share their knowledge and life experiences with others. Real leaders rise up when needed, and they are never complacent sitting on the sidelines. Leadership is not something that you can teach because those that are leaders are born with the skill trait. Those that have true leadership skills have it embedded deep within the core of their personality. A leader is one that others wants to imitate and are often the ones that can draw other people in. There are so many people that desire to lead, but they are not successful because you cannot force authentic leadership. God wants those of us that are leaders to take a stand and let our lights shine. Leaders never fade into the background because that was never the intention. Once you decide to lead, you will experience the grace to be the example that God demands and also the joy that comes with knowing that you are impacting lives.

What's in Your Hands?

As good servant managers of God's grace in its various forms, serve one another with the gift each of you has received. (1 Peter 4:10)

We all have a special gift that is embedded deep within us before birth. Unfortunately, so many do not recognize or try to use those gifts. Do you know what your gifts are? You can first determine what your gifts are by recognizing what you are good at. What if your gift can be used to touch lives? What if you realizing your potential stems from your acknowledgement that you have a unique opportunity to do something different with your life. There comes a point in life that you have to acknowledge that your life is greater than you. There is a gift in your hands that can be used to encourage and help someone else. Using your God-given gifts requires a sacrifice and humbling of oneself. You must recognize that your life is not about you at all. Your life's purpose is to be used to edify God and to be His hands and feet throughout the Earth. When you want to give up utilizing your gifts, just remember that someone else is depending on your obedience. Someone needs a reason to hold on and to keep fighting. Someone out there will be blessed by what it is in your hands. You cannot compare your gift to that of others because it is uniquely yours. Do not bury your gift out of fear of being understood or accepted. If used properly, your gift will not only bless others, but it will be a blessing to you.

Peace Be Still

I have told you these things, so that in me you may have peace. In this world you will have trouble. But take heart! I have overcome the world. (John 16:33)

It is so comforting to know that our Heavenly Father is already aware of the situations that concern us. I often remind God that all He has to do is speak one word to my circumstances: "Peace." Recognize and acknowledge that if He has allowed you to experience the "valleys," He will lead you right through it. You do not have to fear or worry. It may seem as if the trial is too hard and too overwhelming, but please know that God has not forsaken you. He wants to handle our burdens. If we pray about it, we must have assurance that God does indeed hear our prayers. Faith is not believing when the times are good. Faith is believing that those unspoken prayer requests are going to manifest into reality. Faith is saying, "God, I trust you even when it seems like this burden is too heavy. Lord, speak peace into my situation, and I give it over to you." Impossibilities become null when we give them to God.

Proper Planning

Put God in charge of your work, then what you've planned will take place. (Proverbs 16:3)

I am an advocate for planning. Being meticulous about details can be so exhausting, but it can ensure success when you have long-term goals in mind. I have so many big ideas and aspirations, but I am careful that I do not neglect to consider what God wants for me and His ultimate Will for my life. It is asinine to think that you can experience success in this life simply based on your own merit and abilities. We sometimes can be the hindrance to our own achievement because we refuse to seek God for direction. Do not be so overzealous about what you want to do, where you want to go, and how you want to get there that you begin to rely on your own ability and strength. There is a great blessing in releasing the reins of your plans and giving them to God. No one can stop what He starts, and if He opens a door, no one can shut it. Give your plans to Him and allow Him to lead you. Always remember that He sees the end from the beginning! He will never fail you. We all need help at some time in our lives. There is no greater source of help than our Lord.

Be Free

Stripping off every unnecessary weight and the sin which so easily and cleverly entangles us, let us run with endurance and active persistence the race that is set before us. (Hebrews 12:1)

You might be prevented from going to the next level because you have over-packed. You are weighed down because you are trying to take dead relationships, jealousy, bitterness, anger, worry, and resentment with you. You will have to lighten your load to continue on your journey. So you may wonder how to become free. Think of your life like a suitcase that you pack for a trip. You add all kinds of items that you think you may need while you are away from home. How many times do you go back into that suitcase and remove unnecessary items before you leave for your destination? We should take the time to evaluate our lives the same way. Do you really need to hold on to that anger? Is that relationship really as healthy as it could be? Are certain things that you are exposing yourself to triggering you to live a life contrary to what God desires for you? Are you truly happy with those currently in your life? Is there a relationship that you are in that you need to remove yourself from? There is nothing greater than freedom in your everyday living. So start unpacking today. Remove everything that is not a necessity or adding value to your life. Free yourself in order to be elevated.

When Settling Is Not an Option

*We pleaded with you, encouraged you, and urged you
to live your lives in a way that God would consider
worthy. For he called you to share in his Kingdom
and glory. (1 Thessalonians 2:12)*

It is unfortunate that sometimes those that are in our inner circle
are not breathing life into us but instead death. The company
that we entertain and keep can sometimes be bad influences
that we keep around because of convenience. Never settle! So many
times we hold on to people that we should have let go of long ago.
We become complacent because we choose to overlook the warning
signs, and we willingly accept less than what we deserve. We can hinder our blessings and miss opportunities to experience the next level
by being unwilling to disconnect. It is because of these relationships
that you might experience being stagnant and stuck. If you know
that what you are in and who you are in a relationship with is not
what you want, let it go. This applies to all types of relationships.
Always choose peace over temporary happiness. You get to decide
what you are willing to accept. You are the only one in control of
your happiness, joy, and peace. Make the right choice for you!

About the Author

ndrea Curry, MHA, PhD is a native of Memphis, Tennessee. She earned her bachelor of science degree from Christian Brothers University in 2005. In 2015, she graduated as summa cum laude from Walden University as she received her master of healthcare administration degree. Andrea has always had high aspirations for herself, and hard work has never been a deterrent for reaching her goals. So while finishing her doctor of philosophy dissertation, she felt that it was time to publish her first book. She has been told by many that she consistently delivers timely messages that encourage others to not give up. Andrea has a servant's heart which is evident in how she loves God and treats others. She has not allowed the heartbreaks of life to dampen her resolve to accomplish her goals and to move forward. It is her hope that the messages that she shares will touch lives all over the world and allow the bright light that she possesses to reach all that would embrace it. Andrea is an advocate for faith walking and often quotes Hebrews 11:1, which says, "Now faith is the substance of things hoped for, the evidence of things not seen." She has walked by faith with each venture, and God has been faithful. She truly believes that this is only the beginning of her literary career.

CPSIA information can be obtained
at www.ICGtesting.com
Printed in the USA
LVHW090812270119
605398LV00001BB/174/P

9 781644 167762